MY GIRL POWER JOURNAL

by SARAH PARVIS

CREATE

CELEBRATE

Contemplate

downtown bookworks

downtown bookworks

Downtown Bookworks Inc.
265 Canal Street
New York, NY 10013
www.downtownbookworks.com

Illustrations by Scott Kolins: pages 5 (Bumblebee), 8, 15, 22, 30, 44,
54–55 (Bumblebee, Katana, Starfire), 61, 74, 94, 95, 96, 114–115,
122 (Bumblebee), 134 (Bumblebee), 150, 160 (Bumblebee, Katana, Starfire),
back cover (Bumblebee, Raven, Katana).

Designed by Georgia Rucker

Printed in China
September 2017

ISBN: 9781941367346

10 9 8 7 6 5 4 3 2 1

THIS BOOK
IS THE PROPERTY OF,
AND IS FILLED WITH THE
AMAZING, CREATIVE
THOUGHTS OF

_____

Super heroes have amazing abilities. Some have super-strength or super-speed or the ability to fly. You have amazing abilities too—to be kind and compassionate, to stand up for what you believe in, to come up with great ideas for books or movies or skyscrapers. You have a busy life with ups and downs. You have feelings and opinions that shape your world, and you dream big dreams about the future.

In the pages of this journal, there are prompts and spaces to doodle or write

POWER

out your thoughts. What would the world be like if you could fly? Or teleport? Or make creatures out of water? Think about the things that make you happy or sad, the adventures you hope to go on someday, the people who inspire you, the machines you'd like to invent, and start writing. There are no right or wrong answers, just space to explore your power—to create, celebrate, and contemplate. Your journey starts NOW. Enjoy!

My name is _____ .

My favorite hobby is _____ .

These are the people who make up my family and close friends:

The thing that makes me happiest is:

I want to know more about:

If I moved away tomorrow, I would want my classmates to remember these things about me:

Batgirl is a martial arts whiz, and she uses her skills to subdue any super-villains who get in her way. When she's not protecting people, fighting crime, or zooming around Gotham City on her motorcycle, she is a librarian. She uses her smarts and her access to the city's documents to stay prepared for any challenge that comes her way. She even memorizes maps of the city and blueprints of buildings so she'll know the best way to sneak up on any super-villain.

I don't spend my days reading blueprints, but I have some special knowledge that would come in handy when battling bad guys. I know a lot about:

Every super hero is different. They have different skills, powers, experiences, and personalities.

I am one-of-a-kind because:

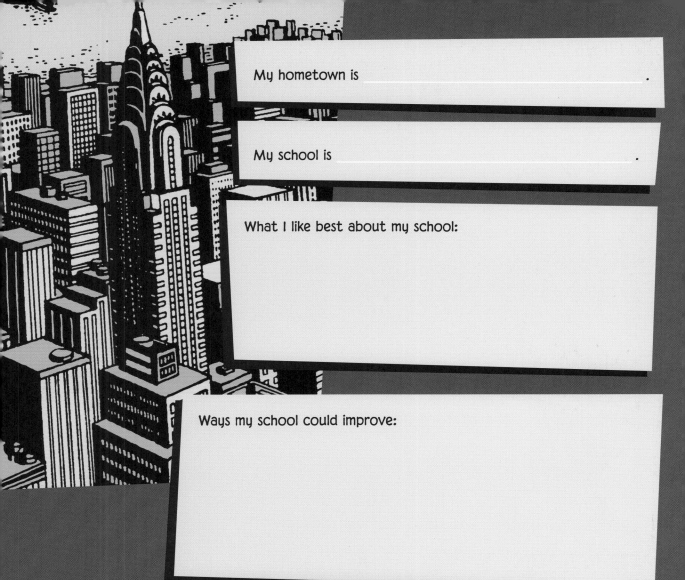

My hometown is _____.

My school is _____.

What I like best about my school:

Ways my school could improve:

Sometimes, we take time out of class for assemblies and other events. This is the one I liked best (and why):

WORDS CAN LEVEL THE MIGHTIEST OF MOUNTAINS.

A quotation that inspires me is:

"

"

My favorite line from a movie is:

"

"

If I could make one rule that everyone in the world had to follow, it would be:

Pick one word that brings you joy. Write that word in BIG BLOCK LETTERS. Color in the letters and decorate the word with doodles and embellishments.

The best advice I ever got was:

The best advice I ever gave was:

HONESTY IS MY
POLICY.

Sometimes, it's best to just listen. I am a good listener, especially when I am with

_____ .

If I could shout one thing to the world, it would be:

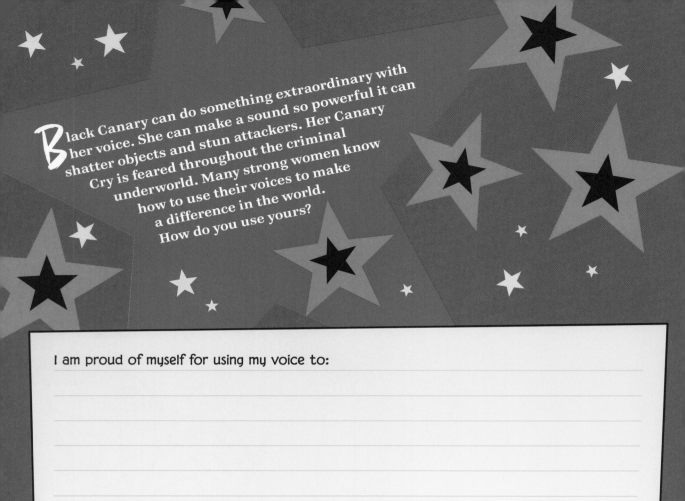

Black Canary can do something extraordinary with her voice. She can make a sound so powerful it can shatter objects and stun attackers. Her Canary Cry is feared throughout the criminal underworld. Many strong women know how to use their voices to make a difference in the world. How do you use yours?

I am proud of myself for using my voice to:

_____

_____

_____

_____

_____

_____

_____

Once I stood up to a bully. This is what I said:

_____

_____

_____

_____

_____

_____

LIFT YOUR VOICE!

This is something I WISH I had said to someone who was being unkind:

_____

_____

_____

_____

_____

_____

_____

Black Canary's cry is so piercing it can break apart metal. If I had that kind of power, I would use it only if:

_____

_____

_____

_____

_____

5 wishes I'd love to come true:

What I'd buy with $1 million:

My ideal 16th birthday party:

people who always make me laugh:

Wonder Woman grew up on a peaceful island along with other exceptionally strong women called Amazons. She has used her super-strength to defeat super-villains from Cheetah to Doomsday to the evil sorceress Circe. She can outrun a speeding train and play tug-of-war with a dinosaur—and win.

I may not be an Amazon, but I am tough.
These are things I do that make me feel strong:

This is a situation I handled like a super hero:

Here is a situation I could have handled a little better:

BE CREATIVE. BE ADVENTUROUS.
BE ORIGINAL.

Super-smart scientist Karen Beecher built an incredible, high-tech, solar-powered super hero suit. When she wears the suit, she becomes Bumblebee. She can shrink down to the size of a bee, fly around, and move with superhuman agility. Her helmet harnesses electricity and solar power so she can shoot out energy "stings."

DREAM IT! BUILD IT!

If I designed my own super hero suit, it would give me the power to:

Shoot water, fire, Ice and lave

This is what my FABULOUS super hero suit would look like
(complete with built-in tools and gadgets!):

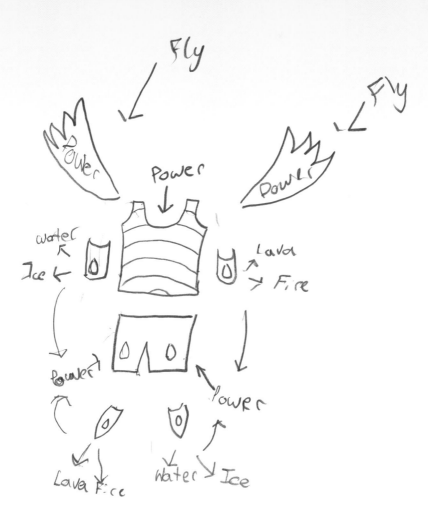

S   M   T   W   T   F   S

My favorite holiday is:

The silliest holiday is:

Here are 3 holidays I would create if I were in charge:

The best gift I ever received was:

The gift I am most proud of giving is:

_____ is someone who totally deserves to get a present.

Here's a gift I would like to give to a friend:

If I saw a stranger having a really bad day, I would give him or her:

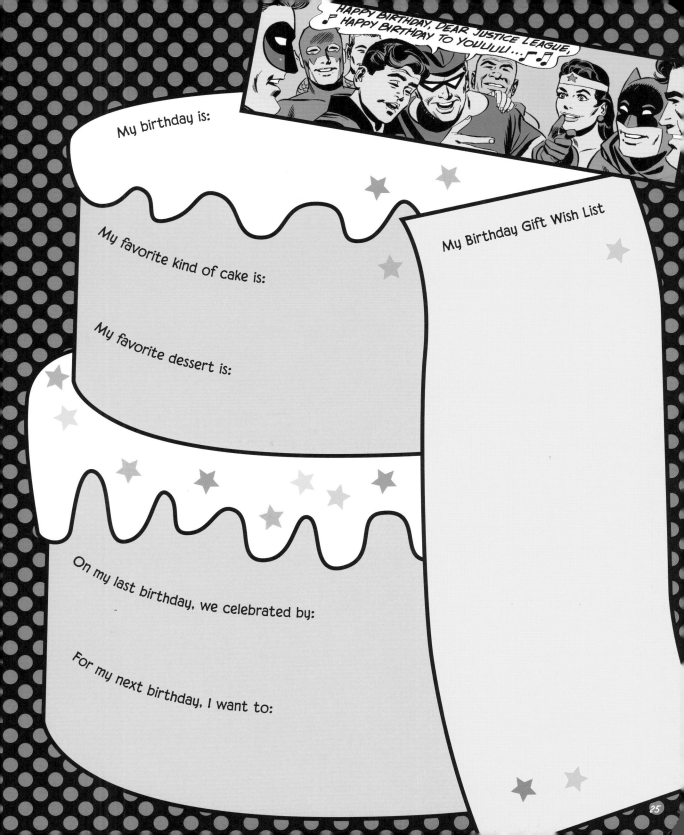

My birthday is:

My favorite kind of cake is:

My favorite dessert is:

My Birthday Gift Wish List

On my last birthday, we celebrated by:

For my next birthday, I want to:

25

Supergirl is not from the planet Earth. She is from Krypton. She came to this planet as a teenager. She didn't know anyone at all. Talk about being the new kid on the block!

On my first day at a new school, I felt:

Here's what happened that day:

The first person I met at my school was _____ .

My new classmates made me feel welcome when they:

When I meet new students, I try to make them feel comfortable by:

Sometimes Supergirl feels like an outsider. Everybody feels that way sometimes.

The last time I felt like I didn't belong was:

But, deep down, I know I belong because:

Super-speed? Super-hearing? Invisibility? Control the weather? Fly? Talk to animals? What superpowers do I want the most? How would I use them to make the world a better place?

If I need a good cry, I know I can always listen to this song, or read this book, or watch this movie:

My friend _____ is great at cheering me up. And here is why:

Before a big test, an important game, or a recital, I do this for good luck:

WRITE YOUR OWN STORY!

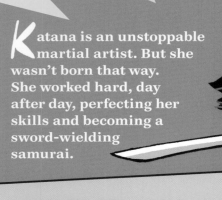

Katana is an unstoppable martial artist. But she wasn't born that way. She worked hard, day after day, perfecting her skills and becoming a sword-wielding samurai.

Here are the skills I would love to master:

I know I don't have to be the best at everything. Here are some things that I love to do, no matter what:

I am willing to work at this skill every day until I am great at it:

If I were an architect, this is the kind of building I would design:

My mom is _____ .

My dad is _____ .

Playing soccer is _____ .

Little brothers are _____ .

Taking tests is _____ .

Broccoli is _____ .

Running a mile is _____ .

Video games are _____ .

Vampires are _____ .

Climbing a mountain is _____ .

Sunsets are _____ .

Watching TV is _____ .

Poetry is _____ .

Jogging is _____ .

The ukulele is _____ .

Pokémon is _____ .

Square dancing is _____ .

Jazz music is _____ .

Country music is _____ .

Honesty is _____ .

Peanut butter is _____ .

The beach is _____ .

Wonder Woman is _____ .

Grapefruits are _____ .

Computers are _____ .

Sailing is _____ .

Fashion is _____ .

Kindness is _____ .

Hamsters are _____ .

Reading is _____ .

Volleyball is _____.

Hip-hop is _____.

The Olympics are _____.

Nail polish is _____.

Community service is _____.

Swimming is _____.

Hats are _____.

Popcorn is _____.

Tap dancing is _____.

Batman is _____.

Roses are _____.

White chocolate is _____.

Minecraft is _____.

Kittens are _____.

Ghosts are _____.

Doing puzzles is _____.

High heels are _____.

Basketball is _____.

Jumping rope is _____.

French fries are _____.

Helping others is _____.

Stuffed animals are _____.

Daydreaming is _____.

Songwriting is _____.

Taking a cruise is _____.

Lobster is _____.

The Loch Ness monster is _____.

Ballet is _____.

Knitting is _____.

Rock music is _____.

After the death of her parents, Mary Batson was separated from her brother and adopted by a new family. She didn't have any superpowers until she was a teenager. That's when her brother tracked her down and she learned that if she said a magic word, she would have super-strength, super-speed, super-fast reflexes, enhanced wisdom, healing powers, and the power of flight. And the word was SHAZAM!

If I found out tomorrow that I could use incredible superpowers like Mary's, the first thing I would do is:

Some super heroes are clairvoyant. They can understand events that they have not seen or heard about. Some clairvoyants can even know about events in the future!

If I were clairvoyant, I would use my power to learn these things about my future:

Some things should remain a surprise, like:

An Olympic-level gymnast and powerful boxer, Catwoman is also a tough street fighter. She prowls the city late at night to keep her neighbors safe.

I don't patrol the streets at night, but my community is important to me. This is how I look out for my neighbors:

These are some of the people who live in my neighborhood:

CATWOMAN

When I get angry, I often:

_____

When I am happy, I usually:

_____

When I am sad, I:

_____

When I feel stressed, I:

_____

When I am sleepy, I:

_____

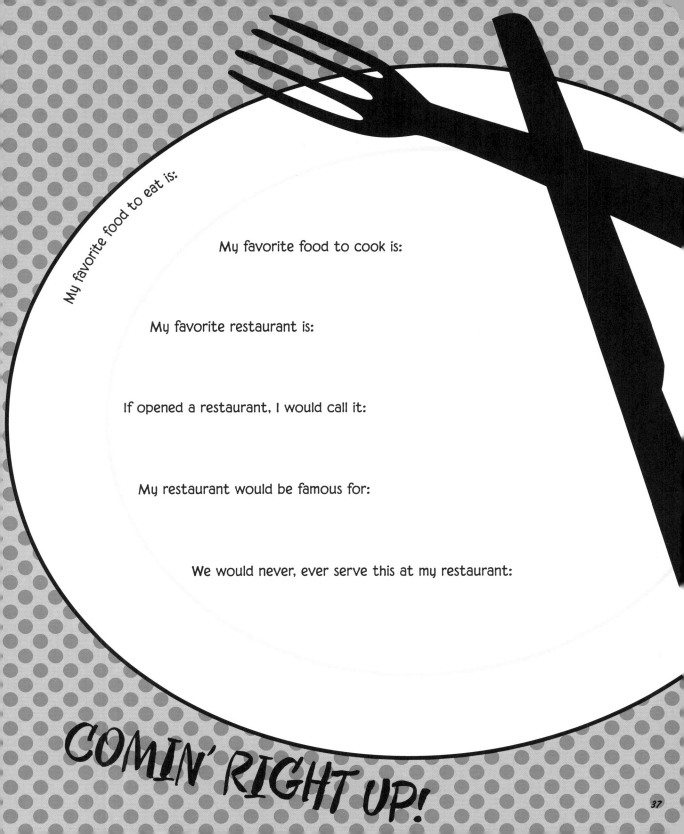

My favorite food to eat is:

My favorite food to cook is:

My favorite restaurant is:

If opened a restaurant, I would call it:

My restaurant would be famous for:

We would never, ever serve this at my restaurant:

COMIN' RIGHT UP!

If I had freezing breath, I would:

The best things about cold weather are:

Gloves
OR
mittens?

Figure skating
OR
ice hockey?

Hot tea
OR
hot cocoa?

Snowmobile
OR
snowshoes?

Build a snowman
OR
an igloo?

Skiing
OR
snowboarding?

Sledding
OR
snowball fight?

Cross-country skiing
OR
downhill skiing?

DAILY PLANET

DAILY PLANET

Write Your Own Headlines!

*L*ois Lane is a reporter for the *Daily Planet* in Metropolis. She is fearless when it comes to chasing down a good story. She has worked in war zones and covered natural disasters and doesn't shy away from following Superman into *very* dangerous situations.

If I were a reporter, I'd most like to work in _____ (city/location)
and write about _____

One current story I'd like to cover is:

_____

Here are 3 big events in history that I would have loved to cover as a reporter:

1. _____

2. _____

3. _____

Just think of all the amazing things I could get done if there were more MEs.
If I could clone myself, my other me and I would do this immediately:

How many copies of me would I make?

But I would do this to make sure everyone knew I was the REAL ME:

5
THINGS I ~~WANT TO~~ WILL ACCOMPLISH THIS YEAR

1.

2.

3.

4.

5.

Starfire can learn a new language just by touching someone who speaks that language.

If I could learn only one more language, it would be _____
because:

But if I could learn lots of languages, like Starfire, I would like to learn:

Starfire can absorb radiation from the sun and turn it into pure energy. With that energy, she can travel at supersonic speeds.

Moving at supersonic speeds makes it easy to get from place to place. Here are the places I would like to visit:

Here are some places I have traveled to (and what I liked most about them):

SUPERSONIC SUPERSTAR

If I start a band tomorrow, I will name it:

Who should be in my band?

In the band, I would be the one who:

My first hit single would be called:

Piano OR trumpet?

Love songs OR party song

Solo act OR girl group?

...ger OR ...mmer?

Guitar OR keyboard?

Singer OR backup dancer?

Songwriter OR band mana...

Flute OR clarinet?

Design an unforgettable outfit to be worn during an awards show. Who will wear your design? You? A famous actress? An awesome musician? The president of the United States?

Hawkgirl was a policewoman back on her home planet of Thanagar. She believes in justice so much that she chased a criminal all the way to Earth from Thanagar.

Chasing a bad guy across the universe takes a lot of courage. I am courageous too! It took a lot of courage for me to:

My weapon, tool, or gadget would look like this:

Hawkgirl carries a mace with her everywhere she goes. It is a heavy metal club made out of Nth Metal. This powerful substance generates negative gravity, allowing her to fly. It gives her super-strength and incredible vision and makes her heal faster than mortals. Her mace can even repel some seriously evil bad-guy magic.

Hawkgirl has a bad temper. On a scale of 1 to 10, my temper is a:

1   2   3   4   5   6   7   8   9   10

I am mild-mannered and mellow.

I'm a fiery force to be reckoned with!

So many people have changed the world!
Here are some historical figures I wish I could meet:

LET'S MAKE HISTORY!

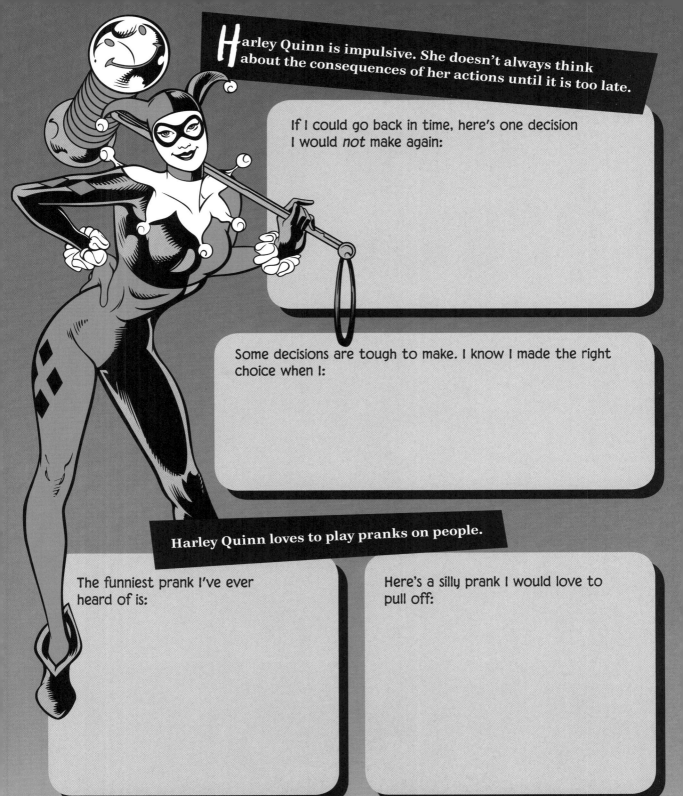

Harley Quinn is impulsive. She doesn't always think about the consequences of her actions until it is too late.

If I could go back in time, here's one decision I would *not* make again:

Some decisions are tough to make. I know I made the right choice when I:

Harley Quinn loves to play pranks on people.

The funniest prank I've ever heard of is:

Here's a silly prank I would love to pull off:

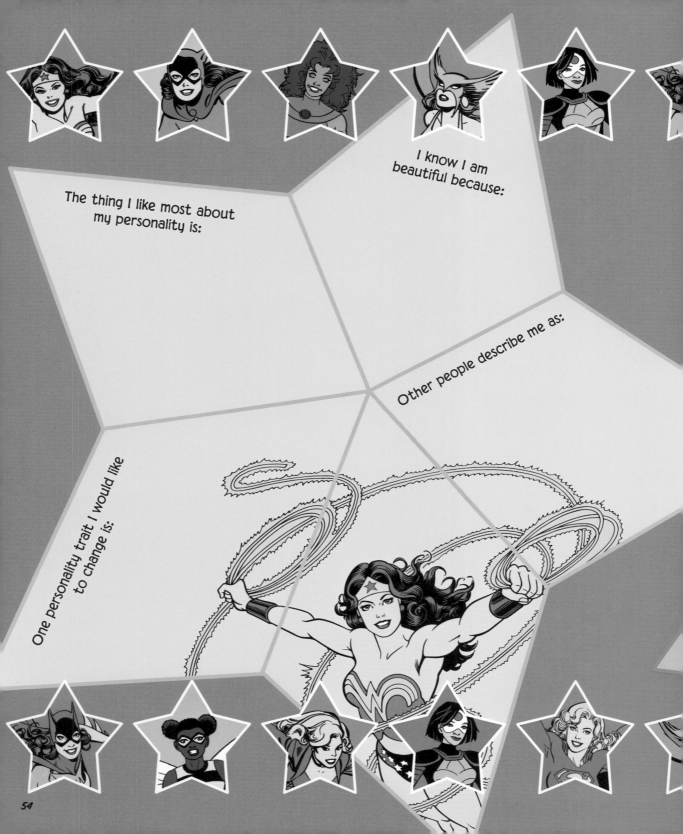

The thing I like most about my personality is:

I know I am beautiful because:

Other people describe me as:

One personality trait I would like to change is:

The last time I made someone smile was when I:

The last time I made someone laugh was when I:

3 Jokes I Think Are HILARIOUS

1.

2.

3.

HAHAHAHA!

Zatanna is a powerful sorceress. She's also a talented stage magician. When she is not battling the forces of evil alongside Wonder Woman, Superman, Green Lantern, and The Flash, she is onstage mesmerizing audiences with her tricks and illusions.

With Zatanna's magic, I could switch places with anyone in the world. If I could be someone else, I would choose

_____ because: _____

_____

_____

_____

_____

_____

_____

If I could use magic to instantly master a skill, what skill would it be? Why?

_____

_____

_____

_____

_____

_____

_____

_____

SHIPWRECKED!

OH, NO! My boat capsized and broke up in the waves. Luckily, my classmates and I swam to shore. Now we're stuck on a deserted island, and there is so much to do! We need to build a shelter, start a fire, hunt for food, search for fruit, collect rainwater, and keep each other from freaking out!

Which is the best job for me? What about my classmates?

The biggest surprise I ever got was:

This is a ☐ book that totally shocked me:
☐ movie
☐ TV show

I did not see that coming!

WHO--?

I ☐ have   been to a surprise party.
☐ have not

I'd love to throw a surprise party for:

This is how I would plan the surprise:

EXPRESS YOURSELF!

I feel most creative when I:

The greatest thing I ever made was:

Crossword puzzle OR word search? · Video game OR board game? · Card game OR ball game?

CREATIVITY IS CONTAGIOUS

Saturday is coming up fast! Here's how I want to spend the whole weekend:

Mountains OR beaches? · Horseback riding OR karate? · Bake a cake OR chop a salad? · Barbecue OR seafood?

Baseball OR Skee-Ball? · Snowboarding OR skateboarding? · Cycling OR jumping rope?

Some super heroes, like Bumblebee and Batgirl, are inventors. They dream up new things and then work hard to build them. Do you have an idea for an invention? How would you market and sell your gadget, gizmo, or device?

Every great invention starts with a sketch. Here's mine:

I could turn my awesome invention into a successful business by:

I would donate some of the profits from my business to:

The name of my company would be:

Actual size of most business cards = 3.5 inches x 2 inches

I'd have a catchy slogan to let people know why my company is so great. My slogan would be:

WORK IT!

SAY WHAT?

Lois Lane is a talented interviewer. She knows how to get people to open up and tell their stories.

Here are some famous people I would love to interview:

I'd also love to interview characters from books, movies, and TV, such as:

If I interviewed _____, here are some questions I would ask:

_____

_____

_____

_____

_____

If I interviewed _____, here are some questions I would ask:

_____

_____

_____

_____

_____

If I interviewed _____, here are some questions I would ask:

_____

_____

_____

_____

_____

MY PET PEEVES

_____

_____

_____

_____

_____

GRRRR! THE LAST TIME I LOST MY TEMPER

_____

_____

_____

_____

_____

THINGS THAT MAKE ME REALLY ANGRY

_____

_____

_____

_____

HOW TO AVOID LOSING MY TEMPER

_____

_____

_____

_____

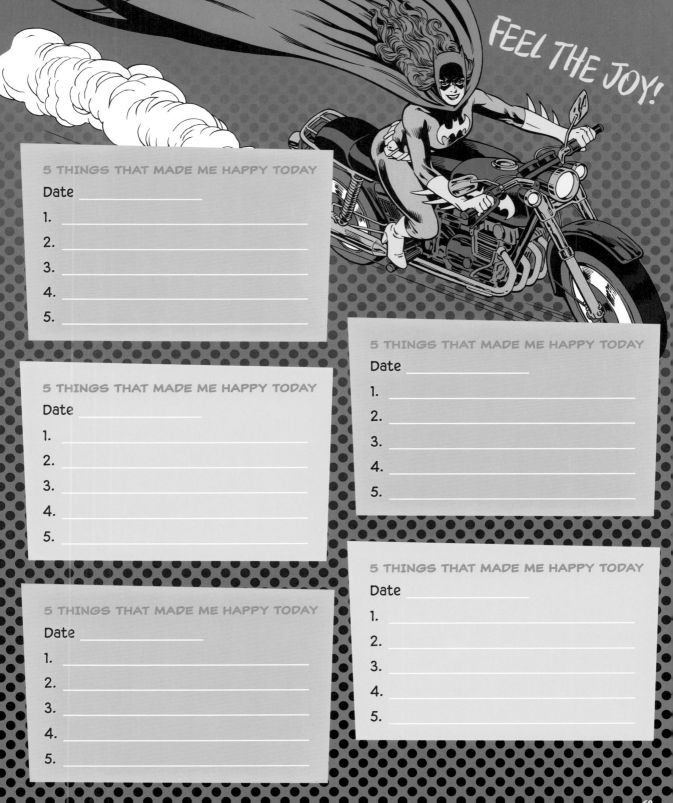

FEEL THE JOY!

5 THINGS THAT MADE ME HAPPY TODAY

Date _____

1. _____
2. _____
3. _____
4. _____
5. _____

5 THINGS THAT MADE ME HAPPY TODAY

Date _____

1. _____
2. _____
3. _____
4. _____
5. _____

5 THINGS THAT MADE ME HAPPY TODAY

Date _____

1. _____
2. _____
3. _____
4. _____
5. _____

5 THINGS THAT MADE ME HAPPY TODAY

Date _____

1. _____
2. _____
3. _____
4. _____
5. _____

5 THINGS THAT MADE ME HAPPY TODAY

Date _____

1. _____
2. _____
3. _____
4. _____
5. _____

Growing up on Paradise Island, Wonder Woman was the only child in a community of super-strong Amazon women. She learned to hunt, fight, and strategize. While she trained to be an unstoppable warrior, she also learned to cherish the lessons of peace, love, equality, and justice.

WONDER WOMAN

I did not grow up perfecting my combat skills. Instead, when I was younger, I spent my time:

....

....

....

....

....

....

WHEN I WAS LITTLE ...

... my favorite toys were:

....

....

....

....

... I wanted to grow up to be:

....

....

....

... I was scared to death of:

....

....

....

... the first movie I ever saw (that I remember) was:

....

....

Wow! I was an adorable baby. Here is a story someone told me about myself as a baby or toddler:

Running for president is a lot of work, but I know I would be good at it because:

The 5 most important things on my platform would be:

1.

2.

3.

4.

5.

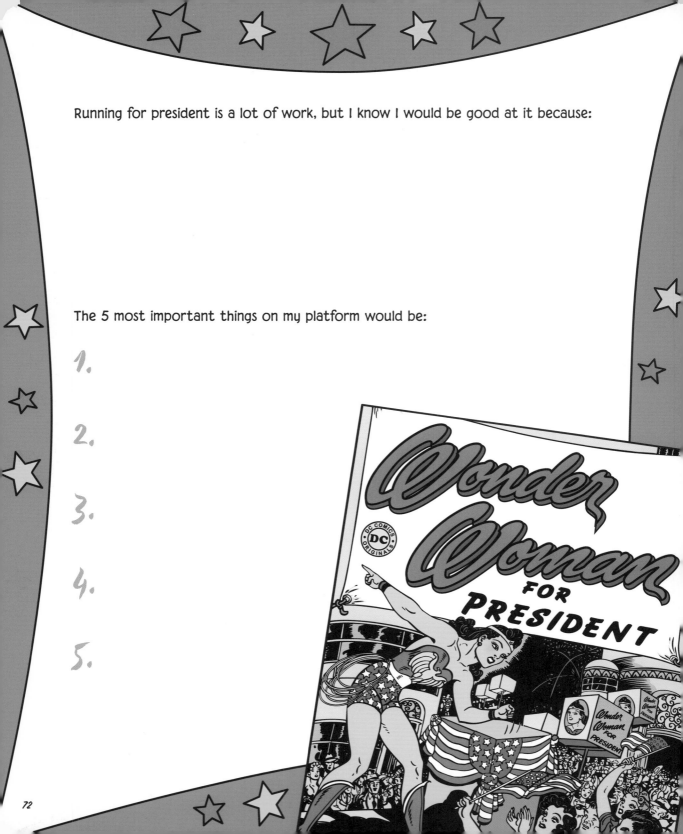

Here are some campaign slogans that would work for me:

This is what my logo would look like:

Healing magic is just one of Raven's many powers. She also has the power of empathy, which means she can sense and understand how other people are feeling. She can even physically feel the pain of others. When she takes on people's pain, she can help them heal much more quickly.

As a healer, I would use my powers to help:

_____

I don't have superpowers, but I still try to help people who are hurting by:

_____
_____
_____
_____

Here are 5 memorable times I was kind to others:

1. _____
2. _____
3. _____
4. _____
5. _____

I am scared of:

I used to be scared of:

This is how I got over my fear:

Here's a time when I was afraid to try something new, but I did it anyway:

Here is something I am afraid of and my plan to get over it:

WELCOME TO THE BIG TOP!

Would I ever join the circus? Why or why not?
What act would I perform?

Acrobat OR elephant rider?

Trapeze OR tightrope?

Contortionist OR unicyclist?

Stilt walker OR plate spinner?

Knife thrower OR knife thrower's assistant?

Trampoline performer OR trick horse rider?

Comedian OR stunt driver?

Human cannonball OR human pyramid?

Ringmaster OR lion tamer?

Aerialist OR baton twirler?

Juggler OR clown?

Ventriloquist OR mime?

If I were the star of a circus, I would want _____ to be the ringmaster.

My circus stage name would be _____.

I would trust _____ to be the knife thrower.

Like Wonder Woman, Wonder Girl has a lasso. Her lasso can make people do whatever she tells them to do, as long as Wonder Girl has more willpower than they do. Having willpower means you can control yourself. You exercise your willpower when you kick a bad habit (like biting your nails) or when you do the right thing, even when it might be more fun to do something else. (For example, it takes willpower to finish your homework when everyone else is playing outside or to wait until after dinner to eat the cookies you just baked.)

On a scale of 1 to 10, my willpower is this strong:

| 1 | 2 | 3 | 4 | 5 | 6 | 7 | 8 | 9 | 10 |

Oops. I always give in to others or to a bad habit.

I am always in control of my actions.

My bad habits are:

I exercised my willpower when I:

If I had a lasso like Wonder Girl's, I would:

SHOW YOUR STRENGTH!

I ☐ often remember my dreams.
☐ rarely
☐ always
☐ never

I had a dream I will never forget. It went like this:

I was at a pool party at Eric's when nana picked me up and took me to a sleding hill with no snow When she took me to a circus. We saw a fat duplicate of bee and a guy asked with a knife in his hand if I wanted to draw blood. I ran a got to Annies house but there was a cafeteiria in her bathroom Where all the fith graders were Zombies so me and annie ran Where I became a ~~muffin~~ and Amie a muffin ectii a Fish

During a sleepover, I am the one most likely to:

I ☐ often have nightmares.
☐ rarely
☐ always
☐ never

The scariest nightmare I ever had was:

Sometimes I daydream when I am supposed to be:

My daydreams are usually about:

HEROES AT HOME

I am proud of my mom when she:

_____

_____

_____

_____

_____

_____

_____

My mom makes me laugh when she:

_____

_____

_____

_____

_____

_____

_____

_____

_____

_____

As I grow, I hope to be more like my mom in this way:

_____

_____

_____

_____

_____

_____

_____

I am proud of my dad when he:

_____

_____

_____

_____

_____

_____

My dad makes me laugh when he:

_____

_____

_____

_____

_____

_____

_____

As I grow, I hope to be more like my dad in this way:

_____

_____

_____

_____

_____

_____

_____

NOTE:
If the adults in your life aren't Mom and Dad, just cross out those words and write about the grown-ups who mean a lot to you.

NOT BEING YOURSELF IS NEVER THE ANSWER.

_____

knows me better than anyone in the world.

If a person (who looked a little bit like me) showed up and said she was me from 25 years in the future, this is a story she could tell to prove she really was me:

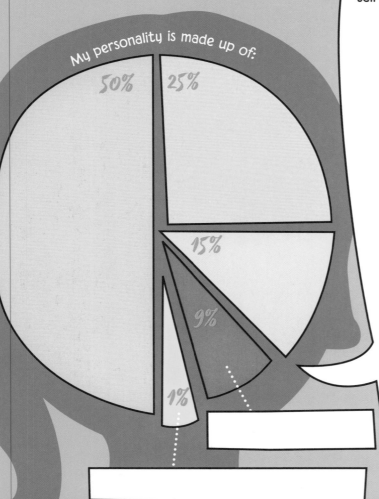

My personality is made up of:

50%

25%

15%

9%

1%

and just a dash of

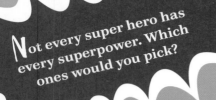

Not every super hero has every superpower. Which ones would you pick?

Control the weather **OR** control electricity?

WHY?

Unlimited strength **OR** super-speed?

WHY?

Read people's minds **OR** heal people's pain?

WHY?

BE YOUR OWN HERO

Heat vision **OR** X-ray vision?
WHY?

Skilled martial artist **OR** expert computer hacker?
WHY?

Super-hearing **OR** enhanced smell?
WHY?

If I were a super hero, I know I would have to use my courage, ingenuity, and strength to fight villains. This would be my #1 foe:

Draw or describe a new super-villain.

Close your eyes and imagine yourself as a super hero, coming up against this evildoer. Write what happens next!

Criminals are no match for Black Canary and her skills as a martial artist.

Black Canary stays fit by practicing martial arts. Here's what I do to stay active:

Telekinesis is one of Raven's many incredible powers. She can move objects with her mind!

If I had telekinetic powers, I would use them to help people! I would:

I know it is okay to cry. The last time I cried was when:

When I need to talk to someone about my feelings and experiences, I know I can trust:

When someone I care about is sad, this is what I do to help:

WAYS TO CHEER MYSELF UP

3 Things I Am Really Good At

1.

2.

3.

When babysitting younger kids, I like to teach them how to: _____

_____

_____

If I could give my 5-year-old self advice, I would say: _____

_____

_____

_____

My perfect super hero name is [   ] .

This is what my logo or cape looks like:

I AM DARING!

As Bumblebee, Karen Beecher is as tiny as a bee. That helps her sneak up on the bad guys and overhear their plans. She's always helping out her teammates by letting them know what the super-villains are up to.

Is it ever okay to eavesdrop on someone else? Someone who is not a super-villain?

Karen Beecher is a scientist by day. Her alter ego is a tiny crime-fighting bumblebee. What woud be the perfect real-life job and alter ego for me?

Mera lives underwater, but she can survive on land as well. Stronger than any human, she has the extraordinary ability to move water with her mind. She can create a tidal wave or a missile with water— or even a gigantic waterslide!

On a scale of 1 to 10, this is how good a swimmer I am:

1 2 3 4 5 6 7 8 9 10

Help!
I'm
drowning!

I swim like a
mermaid!

If I could manipulate water, I would:

Here is what I like most about the beach and why:

My favorite sea creatures are _____

because:

When I walk along the beach, I always look for:

Sunbathe **OR** build a sandcastle?

Bodysurf **OR** bodyboard?

Frisbee **OR** beach volleyball?

Wade in slowly **OR** jump right in?

Collect shells **OR** go fishing?

Read a book **OR** draw pictures in the sand?

Be in the pictures **OR** take the pictures?

BE BRAVE
BE BOLD
BE YOU

As a policewoman on the planet Thanagar, Hawkgirl was hot on the trail of an evildoer who took off through the Universe. She didn't hesitate to follow him, tracking him all the way to Earth. During her mission, she fell in love with Earth and didn't want to leave.

If I met someone from another planet, this is what I would show her to make her want to stay on Earth:

My favorite place on Earth is:

On Thanagar, there are dangerous half-person, half-beast creatures. If I got stuck being half animal, I'd want to be half _____.

This is what I would look like:

Supergirl and her cousin Superman came to Earth from the planet Krypton with some seriously cool abilities: super-strength, flight, heat vision, X-ray vision, heightened senses, and more. They use their powers to keep people and the planet safe from harm.

I truly want to help the planet become safer, cleaner, and healthier. The environmental causes I support are:

One way I like to help the environment is:

Here is my plan to help the environment as I grow older:

LEARN FROM THE BEST

This year, my favorite teacher is _____

for _____ .

(class)

My favorite teacher of all time is _____ , who taught

_____ .

(class)

The qualities I like best in a teacher are:

Here's something a teacher taught me that I will remember forever:

If I were to teach a school subject, it would be:

If I could teach anything at all, in school or out, it would be:

As a teacher, I would try hard to:

The one thing I would never do as a teacher is:

This is what I would do if a kid misbehaved in my class:

To reward good behavior, I would do this for the students:

Zatanna has gone by lots of aliases and nicknames. What's in a name?

My parents gave me my name because:

_____
_____
_____
_____
_____
_____
_____
_____
_____
_____

Here are my nicknames (and how I got them):

_____
_____
_____
_____
_____
_____
_____
_____

Many super heroes go by more than one name. When she's not cracking down on criminals, Batgirl is Barbara Gordon. Wonder Girl's secret identity is Donna Troy. And Bumblebee is Karen Beecher when she's not zipping around in her high-tech bee suit.

If I changed my name, I would change it to

_____ .

As an actress, my stage name would be

_____ .

My *nom de plume* (the name I'd use if I wrote a book) would be

_____ .

My favorite names are:

_____

_____

_____

_____

_____

_____

Hawkgirl cares about protecting the environment. Wonder Woman seeks truth. Mera cares about animals and the sea. What issues do you care about?

Your slogan here

I know I can make a difference in the world by:

Bumblebee, Supergirl, Batgirl, Mera, and the other super heroes are strong, smart, and kind. They help other people and work together to make a difference. They are good role models.

Who are your role models? Who do you look up to and why?

OPEN MIND, BIG HEART

My favorite movie:

Movie character I would like to play:

Movie character I would like as a sidekick:

Movie villain I would like to vanquish:

TV character I would like to play:

TV character I would like as a friend:

TV bad guy I would like to banish:

_____ should play me in the movie of my life.

_____

_____

_____ } should play my friends in
                             the movie of my life.
_____

_____

_____

_____ } should play my family in
                             the movie of my life.
_____

_____

My favorite song:

My favorite singer or band:

Songs I listen to when I want
to feel invincible:

Songs that pick me up when
I am feeling low:

Songs that can make the
world a better place:

Supergirl has a cat named Streaky. This Super-Cat can fly! It has super-strength, super-vision, and super-speed. Streaky is brilliant too!

Do you have pets? Describe them below. What are your pets' favorite things to do?

MY PETS (PRESENT AND PAST)

Name	Type of Pet

PETS I HOPE TO HAVE IN THE FUTURE

I am a good friend because:

These traits make someone a good friend:

These people inspire me to do my best:

When the original Black Canary (who is the current Black Canary's mom) first decided to fight crime, she went out at night in a disguise. She tucked her raven black hair under a blonde wig to infiltrate the criminal underworld of Gotham City. What would your crime fighting-costume look like?

My mask might hide my identity. Or it might strike fear in the hearts of the bad guys. Or maybe it just looks awesome. If I were a super hero, this is the mask I would wear:

I AM UNSTOPPABLE!

WHAT'S FUN?

Baseball **OR** basketball?

See a play **OR** perform in a play?
WHY?

Harley Quinn is very playful. She loves to have fun.

I always have fun when I:

Choir **OR** marching band?

Have a picnic **OR** visit a cathedral?
WHY?

Collect rocks **OR** collect stamps?

Learn about pandas **OR** learn about sharks?
WHY?

Roller coaster **OR** waterslide?

Spelling test **OR** geography test?
WHY?

Ballet **OR** jazz?

Bungee jumping **OR** white-water rafting?
WHY?

Walking a dog **OR** petting a cat?

Play video games **OR** make a music video?
WHY?

Cheerleading **OR** gymnastics?

Learn golf **OR** watch golf?
WHY?

Opera **OR** NASCAR?
WHY?

Science museum **OR** modern art show?

Rock climbing **OR** skating?

WONDER WOMAN

Back on her home island, Wonder Woman is Princess Diana of Themyscira. Her mom, Hippolyta, is the queen.

Sure, some princesses live in castles. But not all of them.
If I were a princess (especially one with amazing superpowers),
I would need a home base or a secret hideout.

Draw or describe your "castle" below.

Supergirl and Bumblebee can fly.
If I could fly, I would:

Some super heroes can communicate with animals. If I could
communicate with only one type of animal, I would like it to be

.

Together, these animals and I would:

Raven can teleport from one place to another in an instant. If I could teleport, the first place I would go is:

Here's why:

3 classes I would never teleport out of:

1.

2.

3.

_____ lives very far away.
With a little teleportation, we could hang out all the time!

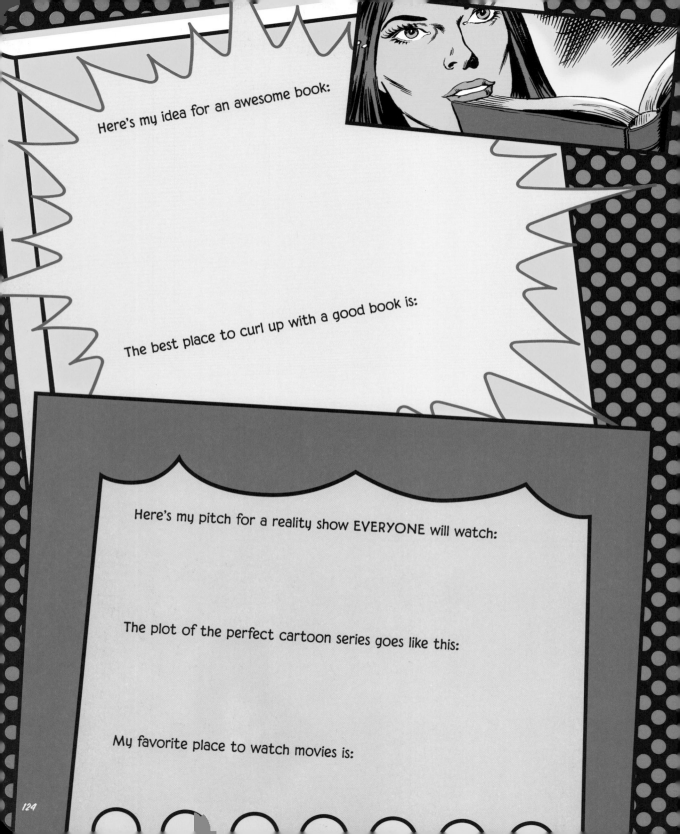

Here's my idea for an awesome book:

The best place to curl up with a good book is:

Here's my pitch for a reality show EVERYONE will watch:

The plot of the perfect cartoon series goes like this:

My favorite place to watch movies is:

Here is my sensational movie idea:

The main characters in my movie would be played by:

My favorite snack to eat while watching movies is:

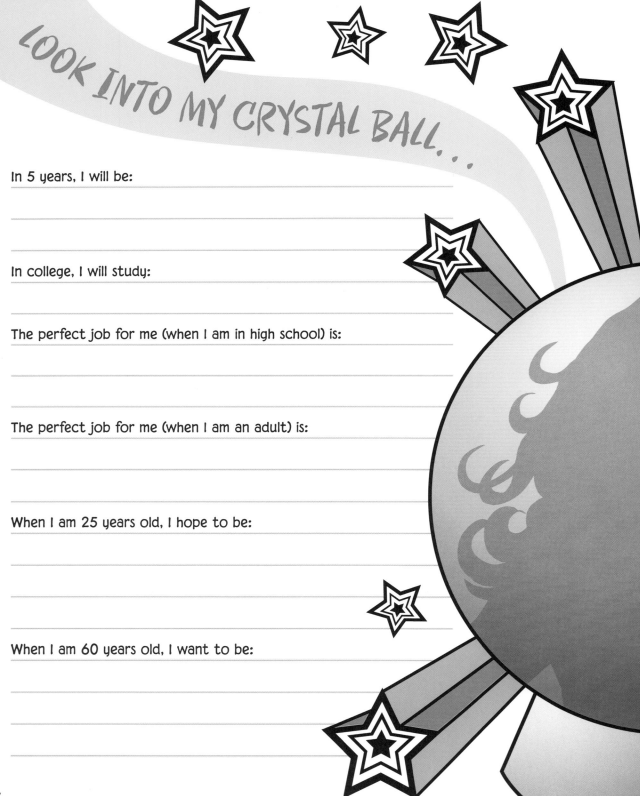

LOOK INTO MY CRYSTAL BALL...

In 5 years, I will be:

_____

_____

In college, I will study:

_____

The perfect job for me (when I am in high school) is:

_____

_____

The perfect job for me (when I am an adult) is:

_____

_____

When I am 25 years old, I hope to be:

_____

_____

When I am 60 years old, I want to be:

_____

_____

As soon as I am old enough, I will:

I bet I have a lot of good advice to give myself in the future. Here is a letter to my 40-year-old self about things to remember and goals that I hope I've reached:

FOLLOW YOUR
INSTINCTS

If I could travel to any time period in the past, I would go to:

And here's why:

Here's how I would change history:

BUT, WAIT A MINUTE! Changing history is dangerous! If I change one thing in the past, I might accidentally change everything—maybe even making it so I never exist at all! But I would risk it all to go back and change this event:

The risks are lower if I go back to the recent past. If I could change something that happened to me within the last year, I would go back to:

and change this moment:

What about the future? If I could move forward in time, I'd jump ahead [   ] years because:

GIVE ME 5!

5 Best Songs for Dancing

1.
2.
3.
4.
5.

5 Things I Could Not Live Without

1.
2.
3.
4.
5.

5 Favorite Items in My Bedroom

1.
2.
3.
4.
5.

5 Awesomest Sports or Games

1.
2.
3.
4.
5.

5 Foods I Love Most

1.

2.

3.

4.

5.

5 Favorite Board Games or Video Games

1.

2.

3.

4.

5.

5 Best Places I Have Ever Visited

1.

2.

3.

4.

5.

5 Greatest Things to Do With My Family

1.

2.

3.

4.

5.

THE ONE AND ONLY ME!

Bumblebee is one powerful super hero—and all because Karen Beecher loved to learn about science and how to build things.

WOULD YOU LIKE TO BE A SCIENTIST? WHAT KIND? WHY?

Poison Ivy was a BOTANIST, a scientist who specializes in plants.

Some people dream of climbing mountains. Others want to go white-water rafting or cross a desert or ride a rocket into space. Me? The adventure I dream of is:

ROAM. BE WILD. EXPLORE.

Something that makes me uniquely me:

A word I say a lot:

What I say when I score a goal:

How I greet my best friend:

How I greet my sibling:

Word I use to compliment someone:

Word that describes me when I look my best:

Word that describes me when I feel my best:

Here's what happened the day I was born (according to my family):

My astrological sign is:

When I want to feel my best, I wear:

In 100 years, I think teens will be wearing clothes like this:

LET YOUR IMAGINATION SOAR

I know I can be a leader because:

Sometimes I am a follower, like when:

When I help other people, I feel:

This is a time when I helped someone else:

I helped because:

It made me feel:

When I need
help solving a problem,
I can always count on:

I once worked
through a tough problem on
my own. This is what happened:

I am a reliable
friend because:

People know I am
trustworthy because:

STRONGER TOGETHER

In her life, Batgirl has fought with countless villains, including assassins, robots, a giant reptile man, Mr. Freeze, the Joker, Scarecrow, and more.

To me, the scariest super-villain in the world would be someone who:

If I were a super hero, I would have a catchphrase. Every time I outsmarted a criminal, I would say:

Legendary magician Zatanna works with a lot of props and spells when she performs her magic onstage.

Some magicians say "abracadabra." Others say "alakazam." An ordinary old "hocus-pocus" or "presto change-o" won't work for me. If I were a magician, this is what I'd say before pulling a _____ out of a
_____ :
(object)   (animal)

The magic trick I'd like to master is:

Growing up, Barbara Gordon loved to work out. She was a talented gymnast and a strong athlete. Her skills certainly came in handy when she became Batgirl!

A sport I love to play is:

A new sport I would like to practice is:

My favorite athletes are:

I like to watch these sports on TV:

The teams I cheer for the loudest are:

To me, showing good sportsmanship means:

When I win a game, I:

When I lose a game, I:

GO TEAM!

If my life were a book, it would be called _____ .

_____

This is what the cover of my book would look like. (Don't forget the title!)

ALWAYS BE LEARNING

Poison Ivy was a scientist who worked with plants before some experiments changed her life forever. Now she can control plants and make people do her bidding. Poison Ivy is not a hero, but she does fight for the environment. She protects endangered species and is ruthless if anyone threatens nature.

An endangered species I would like to help protect is:

Poison Ivy would love to see all of Gotham City turned into a tropical paradise. Here are some places that would be better with more trees, flowers, and plants:

LIARS BEWARE!

If Wonder Woman wraps her Lasso of Truth around you, you have no choice but to come clean. Her magical lasso is unbreakable. And it forces anyone wrapped in it to tell the absolute truth.

I ☐ always
☐ mostly   tell the truth.
☐ rarely

Honesty is:

Here's how I know someone is not telling the truth:

Is it ever okay to lie? When?

If I had a Lasso of Truth, I would:

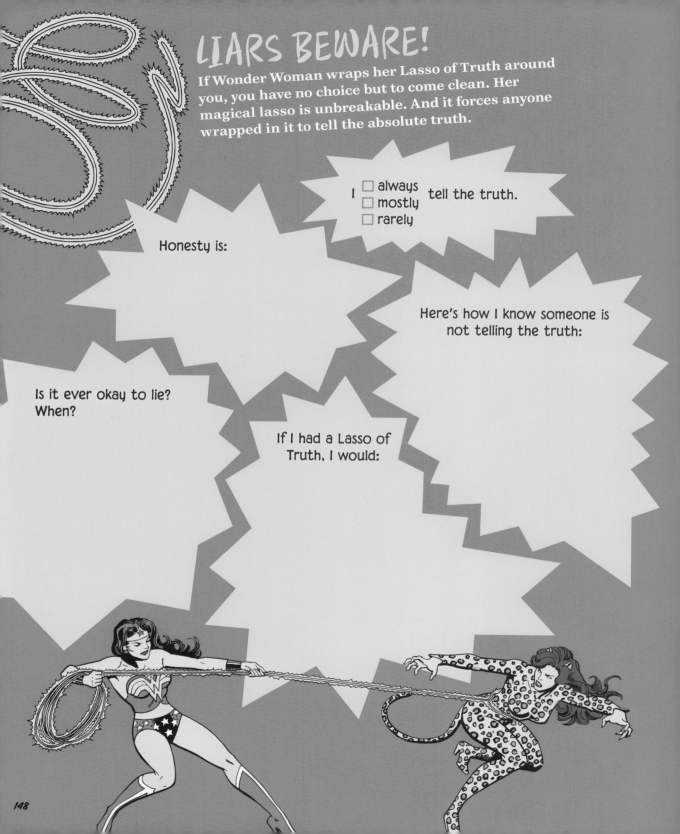

If I could replace one part of my body with a bionic robot part, I would replace:

And here's why:

I would never invent a robot that would try to hurt people or take over the world. But I would create a robot that could:

Katana grew up in Japan. The art of the samurai is not the only art from Japan. Japanese poets are famous for their beloved three-line poems, called haiku. The first line of a haiku has 5 syllables, the second line has 7 syllables, and the last line has 5 again, like this:

WITH HER SWORDS AND SMARTS
KATANA IS POWERFUL.
AN INSPIRATION.

Write about yourself and your life in haiku!

SHE'LL LEAP TALL BUILDINGS
AND OUTWIT ALL THE BAD GUYS.
SUPERGIRL IS RAD.

MY HAIKU!

SCHOOL'S OUT FOR THE SUMMER!

The best summer vacation I've ever had was:

because:

Next year for summer vacation, I want to:

Car trip **OR** plane ride?

Swim in a pond **OR** swim in the ocean?

Summer camp **OR** play at home?

Visit family **OR** have family stay with me?

Relax in a hammock **OR** go for a hike?

Take the train **OR** take the bus?

Go fishing **OR** go sailing?

Water skis **OR** dirt bikes?

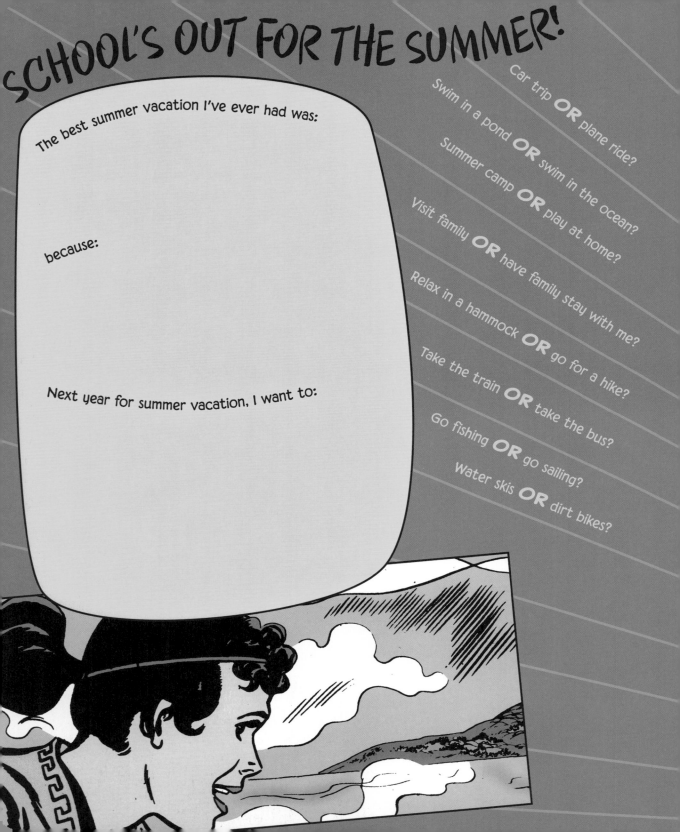

My favorite ways to spend time in nature are:

My favorite animals are:

My favorite plants are:

BE CURIOUS. BE FREE.

Batgirl is a technological genius. She can use any computer system she finds in order to save the day.

I am ☐ not great   with computers.
☐ pretty good
☐ very good
☐ totally amazing

My favorite apps are:

I'd like to create an app that would:

Here's my fabulous idea for a website or a machine:

THINGS (AND PEOPLE) I AM GRATEFUL FOR

THANK YOU!

There are so
many important
people in my life, like:

_____

_____

_____

_____

_____

_____

_____

_____

_____

_____

_____

_____

3 Things I Like About

_____ :

1.

2.

3.

3 Things I Like About

_____ :

1.

2.

3.

3 Things I Like About

_____ :

1.

2.

3.

3 Things I Like About

_____ :

1.

2.

3.

GIRL POWER!

My picture goes here.